BULL RIDING AND BULLFIGHTING

RODEO

Tex McLeese

The Rourke Press, Inc.
Vero Beach, Florida 32964

PHOTO CREDITS:
© Dennis K. Clark: title page, pages 4, 7, 8, 10, 12, 13, 15, 17, 21; © Texas Department of Tourism: cover, page 18

EDITORIAL SERVICES:
Pamela Schroeder

Library of Congress Cataloging-in-Publication Data

McLeese, Tex, 1950-
    Bull riding and bullfighting / Tex McLeese.
        p. cm. — (Rodeo discovery library)
    Includes index.
    ISBN 1-57103-345-9
    1. Bull riding—Juvenile literature. 2. Bullfights—Juvenile literature. [1. Bull riding. 2. Bullfights. 3. Rodeos.] I. Title.

GV1834.45.B84 M34 2000
791.8'4—dc21
                                                                00–022625

Printed in the USA

TABLE OF CONTENTS

MAN AGAINST BULL

The fight of man against **bull** (BUHL) has been at the heart of the **rodeo** (ROW dee oh) for a long time. Rodeo comes from the Spanish word *rodear.* *Rodear* means to "round up." In Spain, the "**bullfight**" (BUHL FYT) often means death or great harm to the bull or the bullfighter. In American rodeo, the cowboy rides the bull. He does not fight it. There is still a lot of danger. Most cowboys weigh less than 200 pounds, but some bulls weigh more than 2,000 pounds!

You wouldn't want an animal that heavy to step on you!

The bull rider keeps his balance.

Bull riding has been called the most dangerous sport in the world. For people who love the sport, the danger is part of the fun. Riders say that nothing makes you feel more alive than hanging on to a bull that is doing everything it can to throw you off.

The thrill of the ride.

HOW BULL RIDING BEGAN

Some rodeo events are taken from the lives of cowboys on the trails of the Old West. Bull riding was never part of a cowboy's life. Bull riding was made as an event for the rodeo. It puts a cowboy's skills to a very hard test. The earliest bull riders of the 1920s used a saddle. Later, the cowboys used ropes with leather handholds and a cowbell. People thought the noise from the bell would make the bull try even harder to throw the rider from its back.

A rider checks his equipment.

BULL RIDING RULES

Bull riding is a "roughstock event." In **roughstock** (RUFF stahk) events, the cowboy tries to stay on the animal for 8 seconds. He does not have to kick the animal with his spurs like a **bronc** (BRONK) rider. The bull is already very active and dangerous. It doesn't need to be spurred. The bull often bucks and spins to make the cowboy fall. The bull might even try to turn its head to hook the cowboy with its **horns** (HORNZ). Through it all, the cowboy must hang on with one hand to keep his balance.

The rider stays clear of the bull's horns.

Making-up to become a rodeo clown.

The finished look.

SCORING IN BULL RIDING

Judges judge bull riders on a scale of 100 points. Half the points are for the cowboy's ride. Fifty is a perfect score. The other points show how hard the bull was to ride. Bulls that spin, twist, and **buck** (BUHK) a lot get a higher score. If the cowboy spurs the bull, the score gets higher. The dangerous ride gets even more dangerous. The rider loses if he touches the animal, himself, or the rope with his free hand.

The judge adds up a score.

RODEO CLOWNS

Rodeo clowns have two jobs in a rodeo. As in a circus, they make people laugh. Even more important, they keep the bull from the rider after he has fallen or is finished with his ride. They must get the bulls to look at them so the rider can run for the nearest gate or fence. Being a **rodeo clown** (ROW dee oh KLOWN) is a dangerous job and one of the most important in the rodeo.

The clown keeps the bull busy.

BULLFIGHTING

Since 1980, rodeo clowns have their own games at many rodeos. It is called a "bullfight," but it isn't a bloody, deadly event like a Spanish bullfight. The clown bullfighter teases the bull for at least 40 seconds. To get a high score he must take more chances to get close to the animal. He gets more points if the bull acts dangerous. Bulls in this event are often smaller and faster than the bulls the cowboys ride.

The thrills and spills of bull riding!

THE LAST EVENT

Bull riding is saved for the end of a rodeo. It is the most exciting and dangerous event in the rodeo. Cowboys risk their lives with each ride. An angry bull can throw its rider hard to the ground. It can also do great harm with its horns or **hooves** (HOOVZ or HUVZ) before the cowboy can get away. Even though it is dangerous, riders say that nothing is as exciting as those 8 seconds on the back of a bull.

The event begins with the bull and rider in a "chute" behind a gate.

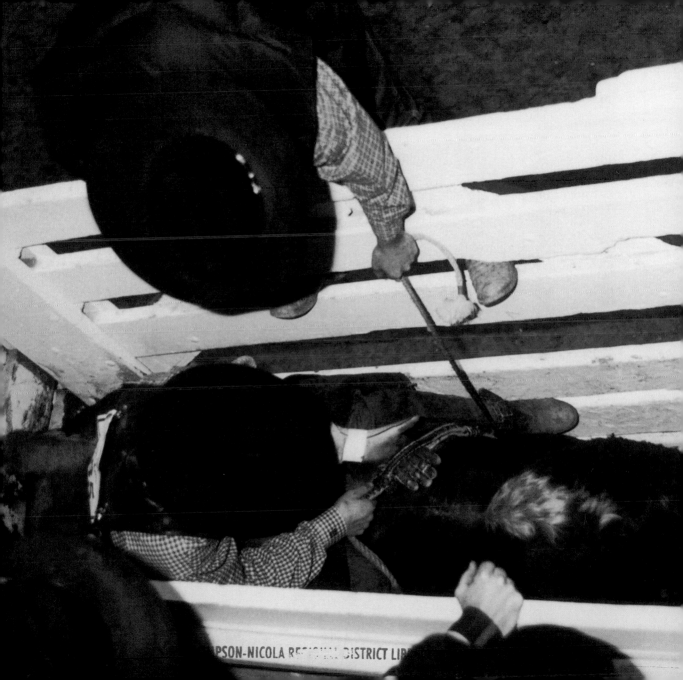

Those 8 seconds can feel like a lifetime. The bull is as quick as he is big. The longer the rider holds on, the harder the bull bucks. No matter who wins the bull riding competition, any rider who holds on for the whole time feels like a winner.

GLOSSARY

bronc (BRONK) — short for "bronco," a wild horse

buck (BUHK) — leap and twist

bull (BUHL) — the male of the cattle family

bullfight (BUHL FYT) — an event where the rodeo clown teases a bull (not bloody like a Spanish bullfight)

horn (HORN) — a hard and sharp point sticking out of a bull's head, one by each ear

hooves (HOOVZ or HUVZ) — the hard bottoms of a bull's feet

rodeo (ROW dee oh) — a sport with events using the roping and riding skills that cowboys needed in the Old West

rodeo clown (ROW dee oh KLOWN) — a person who entertains the audience and distracts the bull

roughstock (RUFF stahk) — one of the rugged rodeo events that is judged on style rather than speed

INDEX